THE PRODIGAL GENERATION

RETURNING OUR YOUTH TO GOD

BY
TONYA HAUGABROOK

A Goshen Publishers Book

The Prodigal Generation
ISBN: 978-1-7370949-3-7

Copyright © 2021 Tonya Haugabrook

Library of Congress Cataloging-in-Publication Data

All rights reserved solely by the author. The author guarantees all content is original and does not infringe upon the legal rights of any other person or work. No part of this book may be reproduced, shared in a retrieval system, or transmitted in any form or by any means, electronic, mechanical, photocopying, or recording, without prior written permission of the Author or Publisher.

Published in 2021 by:

GOSHEN PUBLISHERS LLC
P.O. Box 1562
Stephens City, Virginia, USA
www.GoshenPublishers.com

Our books may be purchased in bulk for promotional, educational, or business use. For inquiries, please contact the publisher via email: Agents@GoshenPublishers.com.

Published in 2004 by The Right Start Publishers.
Reprinted by Nehemiah's Vision in 2009.

Third Edition 2021

Cover designed by Goshen Publishers LLC

Printed in the United States of America

All Scriptures are quoted from the King James translation of the Bible unless otherwise noted. Scripture quotations noted LB are from the Living Bible. All rights reserved.

THE PRODIGAL GENERATION

RETURNING OUR YOUTH TO GOD

BY
TONYA HAUGABROOK

Dedication

To my Lord and Savior, Jesus Christ: all that I am or ever hope to be, I owe it all to you. To God be all the glory!

To my children: a mother could not ask for three more loving and supportive kids. I am truly blessed for having you in my life.

To my parents: in your own way, you taught me to be strong and believe I could achieve my dreams.

To my sisters and brother: although we do not always see eye-to-eye, there is one thing we have always shared. That is our love for one another. I thank God that after all these years, I can still look to you and say you are not only my siblings, but also my friends.

To all my wonderful friends: thank you for being there for me when things seemed hopeless. You will never know how much your many words of encouragement and prayers meant to me.

Introduction

I believe that God's vision and counsel are clear!

He has made promises to us. He has provided guidance about our actions and reactions because they all have consequences.

We can only practice what He teaches when we understand how He operates, and our youth cannot understand it without parental guidance.

That is what this book is about. It describes the three-fold relationship of God, parents, and children.

Proverbs 22:6 states, "Train up a child in the way he should go:; and when he is old, he will not depart from it."

Parents are to hedge their children until they are old enough to be responsible for themselves. Teach them how to behave, how to perform duties, how to escape danger, how to share blessings, and most of all how to love like Christ.

Parents are to instill character and protect their children's souls.

Pray with them and for them, instill the fear of God in them, and when they are old, they will not depart from those things.

CONTENTS

CHAPTER 1 1
   TROUBLES:
   STATEMENT OF THE PROBLEM

CHAPTER 2 7
   VISION:
   GOD'S PROMISE OF PROSPERITY

CHAPTER 3 17
   COUNSEL:
   ACTIONS, REACTIONS, AND
   CONSEQUENCES

CHAPTER 4 25
   KNOWLEDGE:
   UNDERSTANDING GOD'S WAY OF
   OPERATION

CHAPTER 5 35
   RESTORATION:
   PARENTS ARE THE KEY

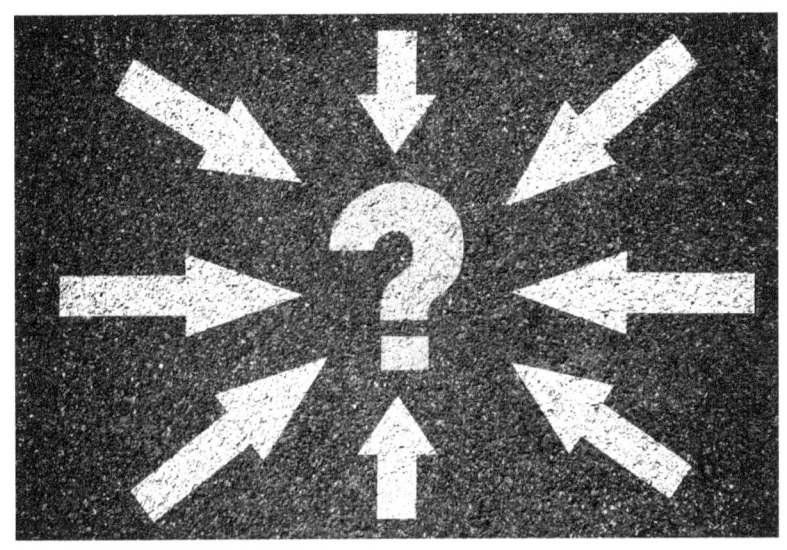

1.

TROUBLES:
STATEMENT OF THE PROBLEM

Every year we see an increase in violence among young people. According to the World Health Organization[1], the statistics are alarming:

> Youth violence is a global public health problem. It includes a range of acts from bullying and physical fighting, to more severe sexual and physical assault to homicide.
>
> Worldwide some 200,000 homicides occur among youth 10–29 years of age each year, which is 42% of the total number of homicides globally each year.
>
> Homicide is the fourth leading cause of death in people aged 10-29 years, and 84% of these homicides involve male victims.
>
> For each young person killed, many more sustain injuries requiring hospital treatment.
>
> In one study, from 3–24% of women report that their first sexual experience was forced.

What is more disturbing is that violent behavior is being seen in children as young as four years old.

---

[1] Retrieved from World Health Organization at https://www.who.int/news-room/fact-sheets/detail/youth-violence

Those may not be recorded in registries, but we see them in our daily living.

They are often disrespectful to parents and other adults, or involved in gang fights, theft, or robbery. They are also complicit in crimes against the elderly.

These crimes and others have some in this nation pulling their hair out, some living in constant fear, and others simply labeling each new generation as lost.

Doctors, scientists, and research experts have spent decades and invested millions of dollars labeling the problems, which they feel are troubling our young people. After labeling the problems with some physical or emotional condition, they then spend millions of dollars in treating these conditions with medication and counseling.

The counseling may or may not be effective in treating the symptoms: attention deficit, low intelligence, lack of compassion, low commitment to school, depression, misuse of alcohol, misuse of firearms, or use of illicit drugs.

The counseling is hoped to be full of remedies with therapy and intervention. It could be helpful, but even in the best-case scenarios it takes a long time and a lot of resources.

Consequently, many parents are throwing up their hands and leaving children to raise themselves. If only parents would look to the Word of God, they would not only find the source of what is troubling our youth, but also the solutions to their problems.

Satan knows his time is short and he has pulled out his entire arsenal in an attempt to destroy our youth. The deterioration of the family structure, our educational system, and the community setting has left a void in our youth that has so many of them searching.

They are searching for a sense of belonging, for peace of mind, for an encouraging or positive word of hope, for stability in their family life, for validation of their personality, for self-confidence, and yes – many of them are searching for love.

Knowing they are searching to fill these voids Satan has placed traps of deception in their paths to lead them to death and destruction.

One of them is social media. According to First Cry Parenting,[2] the most well-known downside of social media is the addiction it creates. But there is more:

> *Psychologists have long observed bad effects of social media on the mental health of children. One finding suggests that children spending more than three hours a day on social media are twice as likely to suffer from poor mental health.*

---

[2] First Cry Parenting. Retrieved from
https://parenting.firstcry.com/articles/impact-of-social-media-on-children/

Their immersion in a virtual world delays their emotional and social development.

Screen relationships also detract real-life relationships and social skills in children and teenagers.

Obsession with self and posting endless updates and selfies on social media is increasing narcissism in youngsters.

We already have God's promise to bless our children. We as parents must simply commit to instilling in them a vision that is grounded upon Godly counsel and knowledge in order for them to overcome the tricks of Satan and focus on their promise from God for a brighter future.

2.

VISION:
GOD'S PROMISE OF PROSPERITY

> *"Where there is no vision, the people perish:"*
>
> *Proverbs 29:18a*

If we took Proverbs 29:18a and applied it to our children we could say this: "If our children have no vision, our children will perish."

Maybe someone should tell this to all the child psychologists and other research experts. For decades vast amounts of money have been spent researching adolescent problems and their solutions. What is so unfortunate is that the answer to these increasing problems has be sitting on the nightstand of many homes and the guest desks of hotels.

That is the beauty of God's Word. It gives parents the insight for preventing or overcoming problems by exposing Satan's plan of attack against our children. Satan was once an angel in heaven, so he knows the power of vision. That is why he and his angels are working night and day to prevent the vision connected to God's ordained purpose from being part of our children's lives.

Satan knows God has a pre-ordained plan for our children. He knows that our children have been adopted into the family of Abraham and they are therefore heirs to the blessing promised to Abraham and his children. Satan knows that like Abraham and his seed, God will reveal His plan for our children through dreams that make the vision plain. He knows that if our children believe the vision, they will hold fast to it and trust God to bring it to fruition.

Satan knows if our children are trusting God, it lays the foundation for another generation singing God's praises. He fears this because he knows that Jesus said, "If I be lifted, I will draw all men unto me" (John 12:32). Satan's sole goal in life is to mock God so he will do what he can to keep our children from recognizing godly visions that leads them to God promises.

How can we recognize God's vision for our child? Before answering that question let us first look at three important parts of a vision: images of the mind, bestowed favor, and glimpses of the promises.

VISION—IMAGES OF THE MIND

The Hebrew word for vision is chazah (khaw-zaw'), which means revelation inspired from a dream. Another way to say it is a prediction inspired from images of the mind. That is why it is important that as parents we monitor what our children watch on television, the social media they engage in, the books and magazines they read, the video games they play, the music they listen to, and the friendships that they forge.

These sources not only influence their character, but play a major role in the types of images that settle in their minds. As parents, God expects us to expose our children to things that will build images of a holy and righteousness lifestyle. "Teach a child to choose the right path, and when he is older, he will remain upon it" (Proverbs 22:6, LB).

Most young people will say they have a vision because they all dreamed of obtaining a goal. I will guarantee that whatever their goal, it is based on the images they have seen repeatedly.

How many times have we seen interviews of upcoming singers and actors that told how they were inspired by the life of a famous actor or singer? What about the confessions of youth in the juvenile justice system? How often have we heard them give a frightening account of how they conceived ideas to commit crimes from what they see week after week on television, in their neighborhood, or in their own home?

What they hear can also impact the images that influence them. How often have we read stories of young people that lost their lives simply because they:

- heard about following the tough crowd?
- watched that fight everyone talked about on the Internet?
- tried drugs just once because of how good someone says it will make them feel?

- shoplifted because of the rush they heard it causes? or

- skipped class because they hear so many others talk about it?

These acts are based on images they developed from what they have seen or heard. What is more concerning is that many of them only tried these things once, and it destroyed their lives.

As parents we must teach our children that the activities in which they involve themselves and the individuals which they associate with can delay their blessing from God. The relationship between Abraham and Lot is a perfect example of this. Abraham loved his nephew Lot so much that when God told him to leave his father's house, he took Lot with him (Genesis 12:5).

However, Genesis 13:14-15 shows that it was not until after Lot and Abraham parted company that God reappeared to him and reaffirmed His promise of blessings.

> 14 *The Lord said to Abram after Lot had parted from him, "Look around from where you are, to the north and south, to the east and west.*
>
> 15 *All the land that you see I will give to you and your offspring forever.*

Every parent should want the best for their child, but this is only possible if we understand the importance of monitoring what they see, read, and hear, their friendships, and their Internet activities.

VISION—BESTOWED FAVOR

If we believe that the images of the mind impact our child's character, then we can see how that can affect the next part of a vision: a favored, fair countenance.

There is more to a vision then just dreaming. The dreams should inspire, edify, encourage, and give joy that is aligned with God's promise of prosperity and peace. Living a life as a drug user, killer, drug dealer, thief, or prostitute does not bring about a favored countenance, but rather heartaches, sorrows, and pain.

The breakdown in the family structure and community has opened the door for Satan to fool many young people into thinking that it is okay to build their vision upon unfavorable elements as long as they can enjoy some part of their life before they die. We have allowed Satan and his angels of darkness to convince our children that since they will live a life built on hopelessness and fear they are lucky to live beyond their 25th birthday, and that therefore they should go out and take what they want at any cost. Their minds have been seared to believe that no one will give them what they deserve, or their life will never be worth anything so live anyway they please.

We must teach our children to take stock in that old adage, "Good things come to those that wait." They have to understand that they will encounter difficult times, but that is just God preparing them for Greatness.

> *And we know that all that happens to us is working for our good if we love God and are fitting into his plans.*
> *Romans 8:28, LB*

VISION—GLIMPSES OF THE PROMISE

God knows us well. After all He created us in His own image. He knows that our flesh can sometimes become discouraged or impatient as we wait on the manifestation of the vision. That is why He occasionally gives a glimpse of the promises associated with the vision.

Take for example, Abraham. After years of going childless he began to think that he would have to name Eliezar, his servant, as his heir (Genesis 15:2-4). God showed Abraham a glimpse of the promise he made with him when He told Abraham his seed, like the stars, would be too many to count. After seeing that glimpse of God's promise, the Word tells us "And he believed in the Lord; and He counted it to him for righteousness" (Genesis 15:1-6).

If you want a younger witness, let us look at Joseph. God showed Joseph at a young age that he would be a great ruler and like his forefathers before him, he believed and trusted that God would fulfill that promise at His [God's] appointed time. It was the glimpses of the promise that reassured Joseph to stand strong in midst of all the adversity he encountered knowing that God's promise to him could not fail.

I do not doubt that during his time in jail that Joseph never forgot the glimpses of God's promise and that gave him the strength to not focus on the obstacles Satan had placed in his path and stay focused on God's promise to him.

The story of Joseph should be an inspiration to all youth (Genesis 37:1-36; 39:1-50). He was separated from his country, father's house and kindred; falsely accused of a criminal act and jailed and lived his adult life in a strange land. Many of our youth have faced similar adversity. Yet, he was able to overcome because he believed the vision that had been instilled in him at a young age.

Joseph's life clearly shows why our young people need to have a solid relationship with God. Satan, his angels, demons and false prophets are working hard to send visions of deception to get our children off track.

If we do not teach them to understand the importance of meditating on godly images, seeking a character favored by God and positioning themselves to be able to hear from God, they will catch hold of these wrong visions and run with them. Herein lies the death and destruction that is now so prevalent among our young people today.

One day I was meditating on Isaac and his relationship with God. I sat in awe at what the Holy Spirit revealed to me. We all have heard the story of Abraham's willingness to sacrifice Isaac (Genesis 22:1-7). The Word shows that Isaac asked his father about not having a lamb for the sacrifice once. Abraham's response to Isaac was "God will provide himself a lamb for the burnt offering" (Genesis 22:8, NKJV). Even as Isaac laid there bound and watching his father's arm drawn back to slay him with a knife, Isaac spoke not a word.

Why? Abraham had taught Isaac of his God-ordained purpose and therefore Isaac, like his father, could see the vision. Isaac knew that he was that seed of promise, which God spoke unto Abraham in the land of Haran when He said "...And I will make thee a great nation" (Genesis 12:2). Had Isaac not been aware of God's-ordained plans for his life, he probably would have been scratching and kicking to get away.

Even worse when he and Abraham returned home, he ran hysterically to Sarah and told her everything that happened. However, because Abraham, Sarah, and Isaac were with one accord concerning their God-ordained vision, God was glorified, and Abraham and his household were blessed.

To summarize, the key points of a vision are:

1. A vision is formed from images of the mind. That is why the informational sources that influence images our children embrace must be ones that promote wisdom and knowledge of God. Hence, we must monitor what they see, read, hear and their friendships.

2. A vision ordained by God brings favor. Our young people must understand that nothing compares to a favored name or reputation.

3. God will show you glimpses of the promises associated with the vision to reprove, edify, and encourage you to patiently wait for the manifestation of the vision at His appointed time (Acts 2:17; Numbers 12:6; Habakkuk 2:3).

4. We can recognize God's vision for our children because it will reveal God's promises of blessings and prosperity that He wants to bestow upon them during their lifetime.

Our children need a vision. They need to know there is hope for a better today and tomorrow or they will perish.

3.

Counsel:
Actions, Reactions, and Consequences

> *"Where there is no counsel, the people fall."*
>
> Proverbs 11:14 (NKJV)

Again, let us look at our central Scripture and apply it to our children today. If we do not counsel our children, our children will fall.

That definitely reveals the source of many problems among our youth. Federal, state, and local laws that were originally designed to protect children from abusive situations have now been twisted and manipulated to the point that many parents are afraid to counsel or discipline their children.

Then there is the influx of child psychologists and other experts that convinced parents their discipline methodologies bordered on the line of being villains or bullies and harmful in rearing children. Parents were publicly depicted as the ones in the household that lacked common sense and wisdom; therefore, they were unable to understand the emotional needs of their children.

As a result of all these heresies for more than five decades, we now have a generation of young people that feel they do not have to listen to or respect any adult including their parents. This new way of thinking has enslaved their minds by making them believe they are free to grow and explore life by what they see is right in their own eyes because, after all, they are highly intelligent individuals too. However, God's

Word lets us know that children do not possess the wisdom and knowledge of an adult.

King Solomon wrote:

> *A youngster's heart is filled with rebellion, but punishment will drive it out of him.*
>
> Proverbs 22:15 (LB)

Paul says it another way:

> *When I was a child, I spake as a child, I understood as a child, I thought as a child: but when I became a man, I put away childish things.*
>
> 1 Corinthians 13:11

These Scriptures also explain why there are so many immature adults. They either refused or were denied wise counsel during their adolescent years and therefore have deprived themselves of not only being taught how to put away childish things, but more importantly understanding its significance.

So, they enter adulthood with an adolescent mentality. The problem this creates is that when they encounter adult issues, they find themselves resorting to the only knowledge base they possess to resolve adult issues, that of a child.

How many times have you seen primary school children crying and whining as they did as infants to get their way? What about those that feel every dispute is resolved by fighting or cursing others? These are adults speaking and acting out as children because that is the only behavior they know. Unless our children learn to change their childish behavior, they will lose out on their blessings from God.

> *Brethren, be not children in understanding: howbeit in malice be ye children, but in understanding be men.*
> *1 Corinthians 14:20*

There are four Hebrew definitions we will look at that relate to the word counsel. First there is yâcad (yaw-sad'), which means to sit down together. Second, yâats (yaw-ats'), which means to guide, or show purpose. Then there is Côwd (sode), which means in close deliberation, and Tachbûwlâh (takh-boo-law), which means good advice. When I put these definitions together and I come up with a question that every parent needs to ask himself or herself. Am I sitting down with my children, in close discussion to give them good advice and guidance about their God-ordained purpose in life?

Early in my salvation walk my focus was to teach my children what was morally right. Then I learned in order to be obedient to God's Word, I had to teach them not only to obey the law of the land, but more importantly to obey and walk according to God's purpose and will.

While my children were growing up, I constantly had discussions with them about peer pressure, their goals in school, their desires for the future, and how God is the center of it all. This is how we move our children not only towards God's blessings, but to natural maturity.

> *1 And it shall come to pass, if thou shalt hearken diligently unto the voice of the Lord thy God, to observe and to do all his commandments which I command thee this day, that the Lord thy God will set thee on high above all nations of the earth:*
>
> *2 And all these blessings shall come on thee, and overtake thee, if thou shalt hearken unto the voice of the Lord thy God.*
>
> *3 Blessed shalt thou be in the city, and blessed shalt thou be in the field.*
>
> *4 Blessed shall be the fruit of thy body, and the fruit of thy ground, and the fruit of thy cattle, the increase of thy kine, and the flocks of thy sheep.*
>
> *5 Blessed shall be thy basket and thy store.*
>
> *6 Blessed shalt thou be when thou comest in, and blessed shalt thou be when thou goest out.*

> *7 The Lord shall cause thine enemies that rise up against thee to be smitten before thy face: they shall come out against thee one way, and flee before thee seven ways.*
>
> Deuteronomy 28:1-7

When we fail to move our children toward God purpose for their life, we open the door for Satan to come in and persuade them to follow the actions that will lead to being cursed.

> *15 But it shall come to pass, if thou wilt not hearken unto the voice of the Lord thy God, to observe to do all his commandments and his statutes which I command thee this day; that all these curses shall come upon thee, and overtake thee:*
>
> *16 Cursed shalt thou be in the city, and cursed shalt thou be in the field.*
>
> *17 Cursed shall be thy basket and thy store.*
>
> *18 Cursed shall be the fruit of thy body, and the fruit of thy land, the increase of thy kine, and the flocks of thy sheep.*

> *19 Cursed shalt thou be when thou comest in, and cursed shalt thou be when thou goest out.*
>
> *20 The Lord shall send upon thee cursing, vexation, and rebuke, in all that thou settest thine hand unto for to do, until thou be destroyed, and until thou perish quickly; because of the wickedness of thy doings, whereby thou hast forsaken me.*
>
> *Deuteronomy 28:15-20*

I do want to emphasize that I am not saying our children might not stray or make mistakes. They have free will and can always choose a different path, but eventually they will come to themselves and return to the solid foundation instilled in them.

4.

KNOWLEDGE: UNDERSTANDING GOD'S WAY OF OPERATION

> "My people are destroyed for lack of knowledge."
>
> *Hosea 4:6a*

The Living Bible interprets Hosea 4:6a this way:

> *My people are destroyed because they do not know me, and it is all your fault, you priest, for you yourselves refuse to know me; therefore, I refuse to recognize you as my priests. Since you have forgotten my laws, I will "forget" to bless your children.*

Now do not get caught up with this verse of Scripture and think that God is speaking to the pastors, bishops, or ministers. God has given us all a ministry of sharing the gospel (2 Corinthians 5:18). These words may sound harsh, but we must understand that God has set the conditions for receiving His blessings. God cannot lie or go against His Word, so we must recognize and accept that God's way is the only way.

> *God is not a man, that he should lie; neither the son of man, that he should repent: hath he said, and shall he not do it? or hath he spoken, and shall he not make it good?*
>
> *Numbers 23:19*

We live in a world where "choices" according to one's view or belief is the moral law of the land. This ideology makes it difficult for children to understand that though there are many choices available to them not all are right for their life. That is why we must teach our children at an early age to reverence God as their creator and sustainer.

Proverbs 1:7a tells us "The fear of the Lord is the beginning of knowledge." When we teach our children to respect God as their creator and sustainer, we prepare them to build a relationship with Him from the heart (inside out) instead of from their carnal knowledge (outside in).

Romans 8:6-8 tells us how carnal knowledge can be detrimental to our children.

> *6 For to be carnally minded is death; but to be spiritually minded is life and peace.*
>
> *7 Because the carnal mind is enmity against God: for it is not subject to the law of God, neither indeed can be.*
>
> *8 So then they that are in the flesh cannot please God.*

When their relationship is based on carnal knowledge, they will not be able to understand God's way of operation because as He says in Isaiah 55:8-9,

> *8 For my thoughts are not your thoughts, neither are your ways my ways, saith the Lord.*

> *9 For as the heavens are higher than the earth, so are my ways higher than your ways, and my thoughts than your thoughts.*

We will continue to build your Hebrew and Greek vocabulary. There are several definitions for the word knowledge. The Hebrew definition of knowledge is bîynâh (bee-aw'), which means to perfectly understand. The Greek definition is Yâda (yaw-dah), which means skillful. To summarize these definitions we can say, knowledge is demonstrating you perfectly understand God's purpose for you by skillfully applying His principles to your everyday life.

Our children pick up knowledge from so many sources such as social media, Internet articles, websites, YouTube videos, television, videos, books, printed materials, and friends. Unfortunately, not all these informational sources are rooted upon Godly principles and therein lies the major problem.

Consequently, we have preschool girls that do not know the words to *Jesus Loves Me*, but can sing songs about boys breaking their hearts or making sure they find a man that can pay their bills.

What bills does a child have at that age and why are we burdening them with that thought anyway? Have society views become so skewed that it honestly believes that it is natural for a child ten years or younger to understand the passion and intimacy between a man and woman in love?

Our children are exposed to explicit sexual content and extreme violence while watching regular network television, listening to music on the radio reading printed materials, reading emails and surfing the internet. They are exposed to violence and satanic activity in cartoons. They see men depicted as being brainless and unfocused if they are masculine, and feminine or a nerd if they show signs of intelligence. They hear biased news reports speaking negatively about people of other races or ethnicity and embrace them as truth, which promotes prejudices.

Sadly, many parents are allowing these informational sources to be a major part of their child's learning experience. Studies have shown the need for parents to monitor these sources since repeated exposure to this type of misinformation leads to a knowledge base that is not only unhealthy but promotes violence at an early age.

We must never forget that our children's eyes and ears are the gateway to their souls. If we allow their souls to be filled with only worldly knowledge, they will be drawn to seek activities that please the flesh.

> *For they that are after the flesh do mind the things of the flesh; but they that are after the Spirit the things of the Spirit.*

Romans 8:5

Consequently, they will live a lifestyle that produces the works of the flesh.

> 19 But when you follow your own wrong inclinations, your lives will produce these evil results: impure thoughts, eagerness for lustful pleasure,
>
> 20 idolatry, spiritism (that is, encouraging the activity of demons), hatred and fighting, jealousy and anger, constant effort to get the best for yourself, complaints and criticisms, the feeling that everyone else is wrong except those in your own little group—and there will be wrong doctrine,
>
> 21 envy, murder, drunkenness, wild parties, and all that sort of thing. Let me tell you again, as I have before, that anyone living that sort of life will not inherit the Kingdom of God.
>
> *Galatians 5:19-21, LB*

This is not the lifestyle Christ envisioned for our children when He went to Calvary and hung on the cross. Christ laid down his life and rose again the third day to give us victory over a sinful lifestyle. That is why God compels us to surround our children with information that builds Godly knowledge and produces the Fruit of Spirit.

> *22 But when the Holy Spirit controls our lives he will produce this kind of fruit in us: love, joy, peace, patience, kindness, goodness, faithfulness,*
>
> *23 gentleness and self-control; and here there is no conflict with Jewish laws.*
> Galatians 5:22-23, LB

Godly knowledge ensures our children peace:

> *"And the peace of God, which passeth all understanding, shall keep your hearts and minds through Christ Jesus."*
> Philippians 4:7

Godly knowledge will give them a Godly focus:

> *8 Finally, brethen, whatsoever things are true, whatsoever things are honest, whatsoever things are just, whatsoever things are pure, whatsoever things are lovely, whatsoever things are of good report; if there be any virtue, and if there be any praise, think on these things.*
>
> *9 Those things which ye have both learned, and received, and heard, and seen*

> in me, do: and the God of peace shall be with you.
>
> Philippians 4:8-9

Godly knowledge lets them know the source of their strength:

> "I can do all things through Christ which strengthened me."
>
> Philippians 4:13

Godly knowledge lets them know God is their provider:

> "But my God shall supply all your need according to his riches and glory by Christ Jesus."
>
> Philippians 4:19

King Solomon wrote Proverbs because of his strong conviction to impart Godly knowledge to his people. This is the same type of conviction that we as parents must possess in imparting knowledge to our children:

> 1 These are the proverbs of King Solomon of Israel, David's son:
>
> 2 He wrote them to teach his people how to live—how to act in every circumstance,
>
> 3 for he wanted them to be understanding, just, and fair in everything they did.

> *4 "I want to make the simpleminded wise!" he said. "I want to warn young men about some problems they will face.*
>
> *5-6 I want those already wise to become the wiser and become leaders by exploring the depths of meaning these nuggets of truth."*
>
> *Proverbs 1:1-6, LB*

If we truly believe that our children's eyes and ears are the gateway to the soul, then Proverbs 1:1-6 should be a proclamation of every parent. A public commitment to dedicate the time and patience that is needed to instill in our children godly knowledge for holy living.

5.

REVIVAL:
PARENTS ARE THE KEY

> *"The just man walketh in integrity:*
> *his children are blessed after him."*
>
> *Proverbs 20:7*

The key to restoring our youth to God cannot start in our schools, the church or at the community center. It must start in the home. It does not matter whether you are single, divorced or widowed, as parents we are obligated to raise our children so that they choose a lifestyle that glorifies God.

When we raise our children according to God's Word, we are walking holy before God, which makes us eligible to receive the promise that He will bless our children for generations to come.

> *"The LORD shall increase you more and more, you and your children."*
>
> *Psalm 115:14*

If we refuse to walk holy and obey God's Word, we open the door for curses to fall upon our children for generations to come.

> *18 And if ye will not yet for all this hearken unto me, then I will punish you seven times more for your sins.*
>
> *19 And I will break the pride of your power; and I will make your heaven as iron, and your earth as brass:*

> *20 And your strength shall be spent in vain: for your land shall not yield her increase, neither shall the trees of the land yield their fruits.*
>
> *21 And if ye walk contrary unto me, and will not hearken unto me; I will bring seven times more plagues upon you according to your sins.*
>
> *22 I will also send wild beasts among you, which shall rob you of your children, and destroy your cattle, and make you few in number; and your high ways shall be desolate.*
>
> *Leviticus 26: 18-22*

When we walk holy before God then we position our entire household to receive the promise of Abraham.

> *And now that we are Christ's we are the true descendants of Abraham, and all of God's promises to him belong to us.*
>
> *Galatians 3:29 LB*

> *2 And I will make of thee a great nation, and I will bless thee, and make thy name great; and thou shalt be a blessing:*
>
> *3 And I will bless them that bless thee, and curse him that curseth thee: and in thee shall all families of the earth be blessed.*

Genesis 12:2-3

How do we walk holy before God so we position our children to inherit these promises? Let's look in the Word of God.

> *That if thou shalt confess with thy mouth the Lord Jesus, and shalt believe in thine heart that God hath raised him from the dead, thou shalt be saved.*
>
> *Romans 10:9*

> *38 Then Peter said unto them, Repent, and be baptized every one of you in the name of Jesus Christ for the remission of sins, and ye shall receive the gift of the Holy Ghost.*
>
> *39 For the promise is unto you, and to your children, and to all that are afar off, even as many as the LORD our God shall call."*
>
> *Acts 2:38-39*

We must turn away from sin and commit to living holy unto God the Father. That was the purpose of Christ's birth, death and resurrection.

> *This book of the law shall not depart out of thy mouth; but thou shalt meditate therein day and night, that thou mayest observe to do according to all that is written therein: for then thou shalt make*

thy way prosperous, and then thou shalt have good success.

Joshua 1:8

1 I beseech you therefore, brethren, by the mercies of God, that ye present your bodies a living sacrifice holy, acceptable unto God, which is your reasonable service.

2 And be not conformed to this world: but be ye transformed by the renewing of your mind, that ye may prove what is that good, and acceptable, and perfect, will of God.

Romans 12:1-2

Our children are not lost as many would have us to believe. We will begin to see miraculous changes in our home when we follow God's plan of prosperity for our children.

And the times of this ignorance God winked at; but now commandeth all men every where to repent:

Acts 17:30

16 This I say then, Walk in the Spirit, and ye shall not fulfil the lust of the flesh.

17 For the flesh lusteth against the Spirit, and the Spirit against the flesh: and these are contrary the one to the other: so that ye cannot do the things that ye would.

18 But if ye be led of the Spirit, ye are not under the law.
Galatians 5:16-18

But seek ye first the kingdom of God, and his righteousness; and all these things shall be added unto you.
Matthew 6:33

And all thy children shall be taught of the Lord; and great shall be the peace of thy children.
Isaiah 54:33

In conclusion, we must refuse to accept society's view of our children that they are the X, Y or Z generation and accept God's plan for our children for generations to come.

It may be true that with all the violence and life's daily hardships that things can certainly appear hopeless, but God has a perfect plan that assures prosperity and victory in every situation. It does not mean that every day will be sunshine, but they have God's promise that they are heirs of Abraham and God's promises to Abraham's seed.

To summarize, as parents we must provide our children with:

1. A vision based on God's promise of prosperity;

2. Counsel regarding actions, reactions and consequences according to godly principles;

3. Knowledge based on God's way of operation; and

4. Revival by letting our children can see us living according to godly principles.

This is how we begin a movement to turn our children back to God.

www.ingramcontent.com/pod-product-compliance
Lightning Source LLC
LaVergne TN
LVHW051513070426
835507LV00022B/3082